Elton John
The Illustrated Biography

Elton John
The Illustrated Biography

ELIZABETH BALMER

Trans
Atlantic
Press

Published by Transatlantic Press
First published in 2010

Transatlantic Press
38 Copthorne Road
Croxley Green
Hertfordshire, WD3 4AQ

© Atlantic Publishing
Images © Getty Images

ISBN 978-1-907176-13-5

Printed and bound in China

Contents

Introduction

It is no longer unusual for a pop artist to have a career which spans decades; many great performers who started out in the sixties and seventies still have that magnetic draw that fills stadiums today, while others who have mastered the art of reinvention manage to attract new, young fans despite the passing of years. For Elton John the truth of his eternal success lies somewhere else. Yes, he still has the ability to fill arenas, singing songs from his "classic period" in the seventies, and yes, his image has changed during the past four decades. But from "Your Song" to "Circle of Life" Elton's appeal runs far deeper and is a reflection of a multi-faceted and polished talent that emerged at a very young age.

From humble beginnings, Elton's precocious talent received a classical training and despite his very ordinary appearance, Elton created an outrageous and energetic stage persona which made him one of the most successful live artists of the seventies. His partnership with Bernie Taupin began with their writing music for other performers and the two went on to become one of the twentieth century's most celebrated songwriting teams. Although the early trappings of fame and success proved too much for Elton, leading to a temporary retirement, he recovered to take his talent in new directions. Elton and Bernie continued to record studio albums but Elton also began writing music for Disney movies and a number of stage musicals, winning awards along the way. He also embarked upon a personal crusade against the killer disease AIDS, establishing a charity foundation which would go on to raise millions.

Elton holds a number of impressive accolades: five Grammys, one Tony, an Oscar, the best-selling single of all-time, over 250 million records sold, a place in the Rock and Roll Hall of Fame, a knighthood. The list is long and is a testament not only to Elton's tenacity and his prolific musical output, but also to his universal appeal and ability to emotionally connect through music. The stunning photographs here chronicle all the periods of Elton's life, from the early years of his blossoming career, through the years of addiction, on to his eventual fulfillment, both professional and personal. They recreate the history of the often larger-than-life legend of Sir Elton John.

Chapter One
Rocket Man

Starting out

Left: Born in Pinner, north London, in 1947, Reggie Dwight had shown musical promise at the tender age of three, when he first began to play at his mother's piano. By 1968, Elton had changed his name and made his musical intentions clear: he wanted to break into the blossoming world of pop. With his first band, Bluesology, he had toured the pubs and clubs of England and had supported a number of visiting American acts such as Patti LaBelle and Billy Stewart. But despite his obvious talent he was awkward, bespectacled, and slightly overweight, all of which made him unlikely pop star material.

Opposite: Elton left Bluesology in 1967, frustrated by being the keyboard player in the background. Instead he began to focus on his songwriting skills while still aiming to find his place in another up and coming band. Although Elton could clearly sing, it was his compositional ability that initially drew attention to him.

A style of his own

Opposite: In an effort to fend off any criticisms of his image, Elton quickly developed a more flamboyant style of his own.

Right: Elton pictured with band members Dee Murray (seated) and Nigel Olsson. Elton had worked with the drummer Olsson in the past, and in 1970 the trio started out touring England, honing their stage performances. It was the beginning of a long and highly successful working relationship.

A magical partnership

Above and opposite: Elton poses for some publicity shots in 1969. On the right is Bernie Taupin, then aged 19. Elton and Bernie met when the two responded to an ad placed by Liberty Records, who were looking for new talent. The lyricist and Elton were encouraged to combine forces and went on to forge one of the most successful musical partnerships of the twentieth century. The two began by writing for other performers such as Cilla Black and Engelbert Humperdinck, all part of their contract with Dick James Music. But it was only when they began to write music for Elton himself to perform that the magic of their chemistry became obvious.

First albums

Left: A contemplative Elton John. His first transatlantic album, *Elton John*, was released in April 1970; it was a collection of deeply personal songs, including the hit "Your Song."

Opposite: Pictured at home in London with his mother Sheila and his stepfather Fred Fairbrother. Notice the artwork on the wall from Elton's second major album, *Tumbleweed Connection*. The songs for the album had been written in 1970, during the creative push that had also seen the writing of *Elton John*, but this was an altogether different collection: songs about Americana, cowboys, and pioneers, all of which were fascinating to Bernie. The lack of released singles from the album helped to establish Elton's reputation as a serious artist rather than a commercial chart chaser.

Applause all round

Opposite: Elton and Bernie in 1971. Success in the States brought Elton to the attention of the British public, and the two were now enjoying the kind of attention that they had once only dreamed of.

Right: Despite his somewhat ordinary appearance, in the early 1970s Elton John was critically applauded as the next big British superstar—his songs, his accomplished piano performances, and his individual and unmistakable singing style brought him to the attention of a music industry that had once all but ignored him.

Electrifying performances

Left and opposite: Live on stage in 1971 at Tivoli Gardens in Copenhagen. It was Elton's electrifying stage performances that really drew the crowds. In this typical pose where he stands at the piano, it is possible to see the influence of other rock 'n' roll pianists such as Jerry Lee Lewis and Little Richard. Elton had toured relentlessly during 1970 and 1971 in order to promote his first albums, crossing and recrossing the Atlantic numerous times. In the fall of 1971 he toured Australia and Japan for the first time, accumulating even more adoring fans.

First Grammy nomination

Above: Elton pictured performing for the BBC in December 1971. *Madman Across the Water* had been released the previous month, to mixed reviews. An introspective work, a number of its tracks are a response to the sudden fame that Elton and Bernie both enjoyed and endured. The album achieved greater success in the United States than at home, reaching number 8 on the *Billboard* charts as opposed to number 41 in the UK. During these early years American audiences proved to be far more responsive to Elton's music, and gradually, Elton would spend more and more time in the US.

Opposite: 1971 also saw Elton release his first soundtrack album; written for the relatively unknown movie *Friends*, the music was a greater success than the film and Elton and Bernie achieved their first Grammy nomination—for best Original Movie Score.

Dresssing the part

Opposite and right: Elton's stage outfits could be considered to reflect the stages of his career. In the early years it was typical to see Elton wearing T-shirts bearing unusual prints, tight shorts, and long socks, and of course winged boots, which added to the effect of his flight across the keyboard when he turned a handstand at the piano. As his artistic stature grew, so his outfits became more luxurious in their outrageousness.

First US chart topper

Opposite: Wearing trademark heart-shaped glasses. In 1972, Elton John's success continued to grow. In April the single "Rocket Man" was released in the UK, where it eventually peaked at number 2 in the charts. It reached number 6 in the *Billboard* charts just two months later. The album from which it was taken, *Honky Chateau*, fared even better: it reached number 2 in the UK, but in the US the album became Elton's first chart topper, spending five weeks at number 1.

Above: Elton plays keyboards on stage in 1972 with Al Jardine, Carl Wilson, and Mike Love of the Beach Boys when the legendary band perform at Crystal Palace in south London. Elton, a fan of the band, had first met Brian Wilson back in 1970 during his first visit to Los Angeles.

Rocket Records

Opposite: During 1972, Elton and friends established their own fledgling record label, which was named after "Rocket Man." Rocket Records was created in order to help up and coming artists to break into the music industry.

Right: A beach pose for Elton and Bernie. Although the two were very close, they were different in many respects, as the title of their 1975 album *Captain Fantastic and the Brown Dirt Cowboy* humorously illustrates.

Born to Boogie

Opposite: Elton pictured at home in 1972. In May of that year he changed his name by deed poll to Elton Hercules John.

Above: In March 1972, Elton makes a guest appearance in the concert film *Born to Boogie*. He is seen here with Ringo Starr, who directed the film, released on the Beatles' Apple Films label.

Ascot Studios

Opposite and above: Focusing on a concert performance by Marc Bolan and T-Rex, *Born to Boogie* included a number of studio scenes. Elton is seen here rehearsing with Bolan at Ascot Sound studios, based at John Lennon's Tittenhurst Park Estate home. The studios are also famous for having been the location of Lennon's "Imagine" video. After taking part in the film Elton and the band returned to Chateau d'Herouville, near Paris, where they had recorded *Honky Chateau*, to begin work on *Don't Shoot Me I'm Only the Piano Player*.

Top of the Pops

Opposite and above: The Elton John band perform on British television for the hit show *Top of the Pops*. The band themselves had developed a chemistry which undoubtedly contributed to the popularity of Elton's music. Not only did Davey Johnson, Dee Murray, and Nigel Olsson play their instruments with verve, they also provided harmonious backing vocals on stage and in the studio. Among Elton's other backing singers would appear Rocket Records signings such as Dave Stewart (of Eurythmics fame) and Pauline Matthews, who would later change her name to Kiki Dee. The performance on *Top of the Pops* may have been less flamboyant than his concert appearances, but that certainly didn't detract from its entertainment value.

Ardent fan

Left: Leading his team onto the pitch. Elton had been an ardent fan of Watford Football Club since boyhood and in 1973 he became a vice president of the club. In 1976 he became chairman (and owner) and financially aided their climb into the First Division of the English Football League.

Opposite: Elton enjoys the training with another football-obsessed pop star, Rod Stewart. Elton and Rod had been good friends since the late sixties when they were both working hard to establish their pop careers. Rod, also a former member of Bluesology, was no fan of Watford FC, although in 1974 he did help Elton stage a benefit gig for the club!

Celebrating Rocket Records

Opposite and above: Elton celebrates the launch of his newly formed Rocket Records label with fans and friends, including disk jockey Wolfman Jack (opposite), in a Western style prop town on July 10, 1973 in Los Angeles. Both fans and friends are invited to the party. After 1976, when Elton left Dick James Music, all of his output was released on the Rocket label. However, following a brief period of distribution by Rocket in the US, Elton's music was again released on the MCA label where it would then stay.

Exhausted

It's part of the performance, but the exhaustion is clear to see. In the days before the high-tech amplification of pianos, Elton had to hit the keyboard so hard that his fingers would be covered in calluses and blisters and would regularly bleed. His performances were often so physical that in the spring of 1974 he was forced to cancel his British and European tours owing to fatigue.

Album success

Opposite: On tour in 1973. Two significant albums were released during that year, *Don't Shoot Me, I'm Only the Piano Player* in January and *Goodbye Yellow Brick Road* in October. Both reached number 1 in the charts on either side of the Atlantic, and the latter is regularly cited as being Elton's finest work. The album spawned a number of "classic" Elton singles, including "Bennie and the Jets," "Saturday Night's Alright for Fighting," and "Candle in the Wind," the original version which had been written in honor of Marilyn Monroe.

Above: Elton steps away from the piano during a performance on British television in December 1973. The now perennial hit "Step into Christmas" had been released the previous month.

A year of highlights

Opposite: Elton's backing band
remained the same in 1973:
Nigel Olsson, Dee Murray and
Davey Johnstone. Together they
performed the hit singles of
that year, including "Daniel,"
"Goodbye Yellow Brick Road,"
and "Saturday Night's Alright
for Fighting."

Right: Seen here with Murray
and Johnstone. The band
had accompanied Elton on
stage during a packed year,
the highlights of which had
included a spectacular gig at the
Hollywood Bowl in September,
where Elton's sense of the
vaudevillian had been given
free rein.

Self-effacing

Thanks to his outrageous extravagance both on and off stage, Elton was being hailed as the glam rock star of the seventies, but it was only a temporary label. Off stage, Elton could also be humble and self-effacing, and thanks to his and Bernie's musical fecundity, they outrode the wave of glam fashion.

A fundraising gig

Opposite and above: At a 1974 fundraising gig for Watford Football Club, Elton wears an outfit inspired by the club's hornet emblem. Notice the insect-style glasses, specially designed for the occasion. The gig drew a crowd of 40,000 to the Vicarage Road ground and, with the help of fellow football enthusiast Rod Stewart, Elton succeeded in pulling the club out of debt. Although Elton confessed to having found his time on the board at Watford to be somewhat challenging, he always took his role seriously. The fundraiser was a critical success too and his cover version of The Beatles' "Lucy in the Sky with Diamonds" was such a crowd pleaser that it led Elton to considering its release as a single.

Firm friends

Opposite: Performing with Kiki Dee at the Royal Albert Hall in May 1974. She was one of his more successful signings at Rocket Records, alongside Neil Sedaka, and Elton took an interest in launching both of their careers. Elton and Dee would duet on the smash hit "Don't Go Breaking My Heart" in 1976.

Above: Elton and Bernie in 1974. Their music continued to please more readily across the Atlantic in the US, where singles such as "Bennie and the Jets" and "The Bitch Is Back" achieved higher placings in the *Billboard* charts than at home. Part of the reason may have been that in Britain Elton was seen as rivaling the Beatles, with whom he had become firm friends.

Valued at $25 million

Relaxing at home. In the spring of 1974, Elton released the album *Caribou*, which entered the US *Billboard* LP chart at number 5. He also re-signed with MCA Records in a deal that would net him at least $8 million over the coming five years, plus a 20 percent royalty rate, a very substantial amount at the time. MCA protected its interest by taking out an insurance policy on Elton valued at a reported $25 million!

A pair for every occasion

Left: Elton's glasses were always a source of amusement, but they had also become part of his stage persona. Frames were often encrusted with rhinestones, and shaped into the letters of his name, or stars. In 1990 a comic play was even released called *Elton John's Glasses*, although perhaps unsurprisingly it was only really a hit in Watford.

Opposite: Posing for a portrait in 1974. Despite his flamboyant public persona, Elton was becoming gradually more reclusive, particularly when back at home in the UK. He was also suffering severe mood swings, possibly as a reaction to the pressures of fame.

Starship One

Above: The location is California. Elton and the band toured the US in 1974 and the entourage of some 35 musicians, personnel, and roadies can be seen posing with Elton and Bernie in front of the private Boeing jet *Starship One*, which transported them.

Opposite: Elton aboard *Starship One*, which was equipped with a piano and a bar.

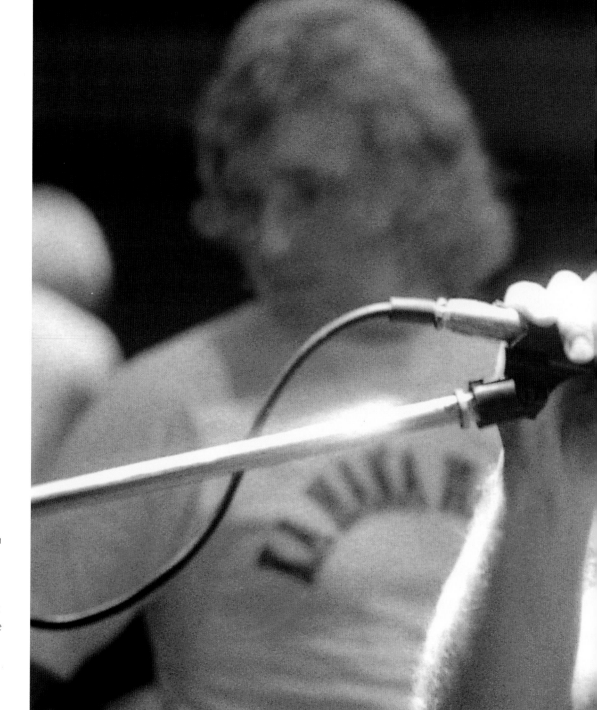

Performing across the US

A pre-performance sound check at the start of the 1974 US tour. Beginning in late September, Elton was to deliver 44 performances across the length and breadth of the United States. The tour coincided with the release of another number one album, *Caribou*, which led to the additional live performances of hits such as "Don't Let the Sun Go Down On Me". But the pressure of success was beginning to show; Elton's famous temper tantrums were becoming more frequent and his weight had started to fluctuate. The US tour would keep Elton busy, but it almost left him burned out.

Hollywood glamour

Left and opposite: During the 1974 US tour Elton paraded an assortment of stunning outfits. Seen with Davey Johnstone on the right, he seems to echo the glamour of Hollywood's past in a sequin-embellished pantsuit with fur bolero.

Gold-certified album

The first of many *Greatest Hits* albums was released by Elton John during the US tour; it was a roaring success on both sides of the Atlantic, becoming his fifth gold-certified album and selling some five million copies in the first year alone.

A special guest

Above: The undoubted highlight of the tour was the appearance on November 28, Thanksgiving Day, of John Lennon alongside Elton on stage at Madison Square Garden. Having famously agreed that should Lennon's "Whatever Gets You Through the Night," on which Elton had played, make it to number 1, Lennon would appear on stage with Elton. Since the single had topped the *Billboard* chart, Lennon surprised the audience. The two had also recently worked together on Elton's cover of "Lucy in the Sky with Diamonds." Sadly this was to be the former Beatle's final live performance—since Lennon was to put his career on hold for five years in order to care for his son Sean, who would be born the following October. Elton John was to become godfather to Sean, in part in recognition of the fact that John and Yoko's reconciliation began on the evening of the concert.

Opposite: Elton seen backstage during a quiet moment.

Furs, feathers, mirrors...

Opposite: Despite the pomp and display, for Elton, the music was always the most important element of his live shows.

Right: Feathers, fur, mirrors, sequins, hats, capes, and even chicken outfits were par for the course on the US tour in 1974.

Captain Fantastic

A decidedly sci-fi inspired costume, but it echoes Elton's alter ego, Captain Fantastic. The similarly named album released in May of the following year is the personal and biographical story of both Elton and his "Brown Dirt Cowboy" lyricist, Bernie Taupin. The songs chronicle the early years of their partnership, describing the struggles and twists of emerging fame and fortune. Loved by many, the album did receive mixed reviews, with some critics claiming it was egotistical.

A well earned rest

Opposite: After months of touring Elton takes a well earned rest in Honolulu. Despite the success of the US tour, many journalists remained hell bent on exposing the star's private life; his relationship with manager John Reid became the subject of gossip columns and rock articles alike.

Above: Elton appears on television with another legendary pianist, Ray Charles. Many years later Elton and Ray Charles would record a heartrending duet of "Sorry Seems to be the Hardest Word" for Charles's album *Genius Loves Company*. It turned out to be Charles's final studio recording.

Keeping glamorous company

Opposite and above: Divas posing together at an awards ceremony in California early 1975; Elton is joined by Cher and Diana Ross. In 1975 Elton was nominated for two Grammy Awards: *Caribou* was up for Best Album and "Don't Let the Sun Go Down on Me" was nominated for the Best Record prize, but unfortunately neither won.

In February that year Elton performed with Cher, Bette Midler, and Flip Wilson on *The Cher Show Television Special*. It was the first of Cher's long-running, Grammy winning series of shows and it was also her first solo venture since her divorce from Sonny Bono.

Chapter Two

Cage the Songbird

A new role

Opposite: Elton the "Pinball Wizard." When the The Who released a film version of their rock opera album *Tommy*, Elton agreed to take on the role of the pinball champ.

Above: Elton poses with Tina Turner at a press conference held for *Tommy* at the New York Plaza hotel in March 1975. Turner played the role of the "Acid Queen" in the film.

Pinball Wizard

Opposite: Elton's role in *Tommy* was really only a cameo appearance, but owing to his position as an international pop sensation, it was much anticipated and appreciated. His version of "Pinball Wizard" was a familiar sound on the American airwaves for several months during 1975.

Above: Elton in a scene from the film. The enormous boots were later used in the "Nikita" video in 1985, which was directed by Ken Russell, who was also the director of *Tommy*.

Clouds on the horizon

Opposite: Only 28 and already one of the most successful pop artists in the world, but Elton wasn't always happy. In 1975, the first cracks began to show when Nigel Olsson and Dee Murray were replaced by Roger Pope and Kenny Passarelli. At this time guitarist Caleb Quaye and James Newton Howard were also introduced into the band.

Above: Elton seen with American concert promoter Ron Delsener and singer Frankie Valli at one of the many film premieres held for *Tommy*.

Twin passions

Above: Elton's passion for football never waned. He is seen here posing with Don Revie's England team, accordion to hand!

Opposite: Performing on stage with Davey Johnstone. Although Elton had replaced Olsson and Murray, he had retained his lead guitarist Davey Johnstone. Despite this, the Elton John sound slowly began to change.

Live appearances were Elton's forte and in June 1975 he went as far as organizing an all day event at Wembley Stadium which involved an array of popular figures who also happened to be friends of Elton: tennis stars Jimmy Connors and Billie Jean King and ex-Beatles Ringo Starr and Paul McCartney were joined by the Eagles and the Beach Boys. Although well attended, the event wasn't as successful as hoped.

Relaxing in the studio

Elton larks around in the recording studio in August 1975. Although a number 1 hit in several countries, *Captain Fantastic and the Brown Dirt Cowboy* was perceived as an awkward album. Its autobiographical tracks tell the story of Elton and Bernie's early struggles as recording artists and many are bitter and edgy. The following album *Rock of the Westies*, on the DJM label, went straight to number 1 in the US and reached number 5 in the UK chart. "Island Girl," the single from the album, also shot to the top of the US charts, replacing Neil Sedaka's "Bad Blood."

At home in Beverly Hills

Opposite: A scantily clad Elton poses in front of part of his extensive wardrobe at home in Beverly Hills. Notice the impressive collection of platform boots and shoes, many of which Elton needed help getting into. On his shoulder is an Elton soft toy. His pad had once belonged to legendary film producer David O. Selznik; part of its appeal may have been that Greta Garbo had stayed there.

Above: Elton dons a sequin-clad baseball suit in homage to the home team at Los Angeles' Dodger Stadium where he played a pair of sell-out concerts in October 1975— the first rock star to play there since the Beatles in 1966.

Spectacular success

Elton really knew how to enthrall his
audience as this iconic image shows.
The two LA Dodgers concerts came to
be considered the pinnacle of Elton's
enormous success in the States, as one
of the most celebrity-conscious cities in
the world fell to its knees at Elton's feet.
These were the early days of stadium
concerts and Elton's success as a showman
helped to launch the spectacle of the rock
extravaganza.

Troubled times

Opposite: Although 1975 was a commercially successful year, exhaustion and tension were beginning to take their toll on Elton. Following the shows at the LA Dodgers stadium, Elton allegedly attempted to take an overdose. The curse of drug and alcohol abuse had also left him underweight and deeply unhappy.

Above: Another friend was Ringo Starr, and the two are seen here towards the end of 1975. They had worked on several projects together over the years, including Elton playing piano in the background on Ringo's solo track "No No Song."

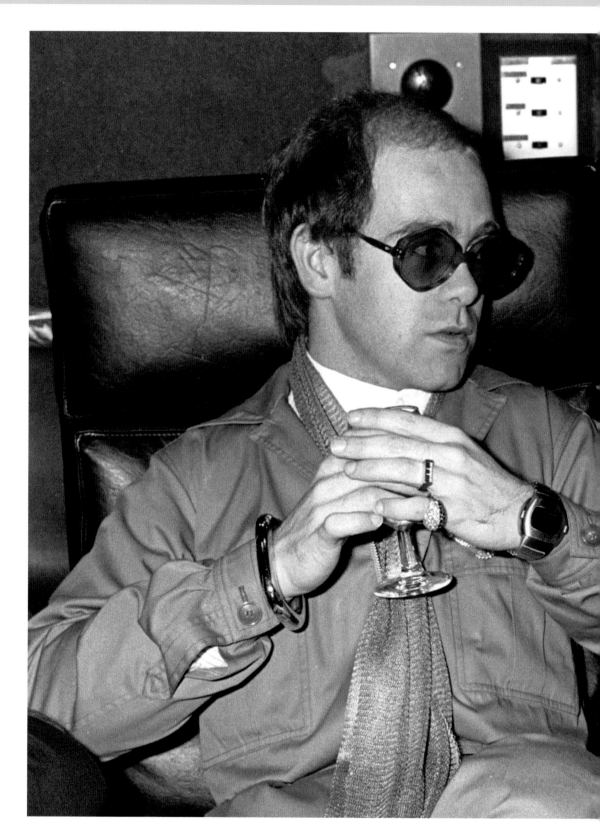

A successful signing

Sharing a glass of wine in the recording studio with Neil Sedaka. A signing to Rocket Records, Sedaka was already established as a successful singer, pianist, and songwriter from the sixties, but his career had been on the wane when he joined Rocket; in 1975 he topped the singles charts again with "Laughter in the Rain."

The new lineup

Above: Elton poses in 1976 with his new regular band: back, l–r, Davey Johnstone, Ray Cooper, James Newton Howard; front, l–r, Kenny Passarelli, Roger Pope, Caleb Quaye.

Opposite: In October 1975, Elton was honored with his own star on the Hollywood Walk of Fame. The event was a media circus: Elton had arrived in a gilded golf buggy and he wore a star emblazoned suit, on which his own named star appeared alongside those of former Hollywood legends. At the end of the ceremony he called out to the assembled crowd of five thousand, "I declare this supermarket open!"

A mountain of mail

Opposite: As he sifts through a mountainous pile of fan mail Elton pauses to look at a card. His star would
soon drift out of the ascendant, however; later on in the year the admission in *Rolling Stone* magazine that
he was bisexual would see Elton's fan base diminished somewhat, particularly in the United States.

Above: Taking a break in September 1976.

Here and There

Opposite: Elton and Davey Johnstone perform at Madison Square Garden in 1976. Elton was still able to fill huge concert arenas to capacity, reportedly making him the highest earner in pop music that year. The UK tour coincided with the release of a live album, *Here and There*, recorded at the Royal Festival Hall in London in May 1974 and Madison Square Garden in November 1974. Although critically not well received it still reached number 4 in the US *Billboard* chart.

Above: Backstage at a Wings concert in Inglewood, California. Elton poses with Cher, Al Wilson, and Natalie Cole.

Blue Moves

Opposite and right: Promoting *Blue Moves* at Radio One, the British home of pop music in the 1970s. This album was darker and gloomier than much of his previous work, its most memorable hit being "Sorry Seems to Be the Hardest Word," but Elton considered it one of his favorites. Some of the tracks on the album implied that Elton feared being destroyed by his own fame; "Caged Songbird" was a homage to Edith Piaf, while "Idol" was a lament for a doomed 1950s heartthrob, a barely disguised Elvis Presley. It was during the promotional tour for *Blue Moves* that Elton announced his "retirement" to his fans.

Feeling low

Opposite: Although Elton is seen here wearing fun glasses and a typical striped suit, by late 1976 he was on the cusp of withdrawing from the touring circus. Despite his continued commercial success, the tide was beginning to turn away from Elton; his former fan base, had been depleted by the *Rolling Stone* revelation and the critics had been more harsh of late. Elton himself was low, exhausted, and in the grip of addiction.

Above: Elton on stage. The demands of touring and recording two albums a year had grown to be too much and at the end of 1977 Elton decided he needed to take a break, rarely appearing in public except at football matches.

New responsibilities

Above: Elton may have temporarily removed himself from the music scene, but his interest in English football never waned; if anything during this period of his life he became more involved with his favorite pastime. He is seen here in playful mood with manager Brian Clough and Dutch footballer Johan Cruyff (far left).

Opposite: Elton found his role as chairman at WatfordFootball Club a daunting responsibility. In the hard-boiled world of football management he was often dismissed as an interfering meddler, but his devotion to the team was genuine. In December 1976, Elton persuaded the board of directors to appoint a new manager to the team and in May 1977, Graham Taylor (left) was signed to the club. Taylor would lift Watford from the Fourth Division to the First, becoming a club hero in the process.

Don't Go Breaking My Heart

Opposite and above: A rare live performance in 1977 of the hit single "Don't Go Breaking My Heart," which Elton had released as a duet with Kiki Dee the previous June. The track was Elton's first UK number 1 single and he had been delighted to finally impress his home market. Although the song was a duet, Elton's vocal was recorded while he was in Toronto and Kiki Dee's part was added after the tape was flown back to London.

A friend indeed

Above: Seen out on the town in October 1977. Elton's drinking companions are Queen member Freddie Mercury and his friend, West End actor Peter Straker. Mercury and Elton John remained friends until Mercury's death in 1991 and it was in part in response to his friend's death that Elton committed himself to fundraising for AIDs charities.

Opposite: A portrait of Elton taken during 1977. This year was the start of a long absence from the top of the charts. He no longer dominated the *Billboard* in the States; instead the Eagles and Fleetwood Mac were favorites. In the UK, the charts were sporting a new wave of groups such as the Sex Pistols and the Clash, and even a the second volume of *Greatest Hits* couldn't compete.

Out on the town

Above: Elton with artist, filmmaker, and record producer Andy Warhol and Jerry Hall. Although public appearances were certainly fewer during this period, Elton wasn't a natural recluse. The party here are seen at the New York club Xenon where Ahmet Ertegun, founder of Atlantic Records, held a party for Roberta Flack.

Opposite: The UK success of "Don't Go Breaking My Heart" wouldn't be repeated until 1990, with "Sacrifice." Here Elton performs the single with Kiki Dee for a TV appearance.

Chapter Three

Still Standing

All dressed up...

Opposite: All dressed up in white suit and Stetson with Bette Midler on his arm. At the same event, Elton is also pictured with an unknown woman; despite such photos, by the late 1970s Elton's sexuality was no longer a secret and rumors of romantic liaisons were scarce.

Above: In 1978 Elton could still be seen sporting outlandish eyewear, but not for much longer. Seen here wearing stylish rococo specs, Elton would soon resort to more sensible shades as his image began to change.

New partnerships

Elton and Bernie signing copies of
Greatest Hits Volume II in New York.
The two remained close friends but both
were beginning to explore new musical
partnerships. Bernie would go on to write
for groups such as Starship, Heart, and
Alice Cooper, while Elton joined forces with
Gary Osborne to produce, in 1978, the
album *A Single Man*.

Back to his roots

Opposite: A group of fans look on as Elton embraces his good friend Kiki Dee in 1978. In March of that year, he released the single "Ego," which was accompanied by an early music video. In it Elton sported a new look: no glasses, cropped hair, and comparatively sensible suit and hat; it appeared that "Reggie" was resurfacing.

Above: Elton's tamer image is seen yet again as he steps out with *Grease* star Olivia Newton-John in 1978. As the year drew to a close Elton was beginning to consider taking to the stage again, planning a world tour that would take him into new, uncharted territory. However, before that would happen Elton had to endure the poor critical reception of his latest album, the refusal by record giant MCA to release the single "Song for Guy" in the States, and his own personal trauma when, in November, he suffered a suspected heart attack.

Just the music

Rather than return to the giant stadiums of the past, the European leg of the 1979 tour took Elton to smaller, more intimate venues in northern Europe, accompanied only by his percussionist Ray Cooper. He is seen here performing at Copenhagen's Tivoli Gardens. Gone are the elaborate stage sets and outlandish costumes; instead Elton was keen to promote that which was always most important to him: the music.

Success all round

Left: Pictured sharing a backstage glass of champagne with English football legend Bobby Moore.

From performing at home Elton went on to briefly tour in both the USSR and Israel, becoming the first Western performer to venture into Russia. The USSR was caught in the iron grip of the Cold War and the restrictions on Elton's tour were tight, but for him and for the hundreds of young Russians who saw him perform, it was still a success.

Opposite: Celebrating promotion at Vicarage Road, the home of Elton's football team. Watford had just beaten Hull City by four goals to nil.

Celebrations!

Above: Watford's win against Hull saw them promoted into the Second Division; Elton celebrates with the team and with the manager he had sponsored, Graham Taylor (front left).

Opposite: In September 1979 Elton returned to the United States for a two month tour entitled Back in the USSA. American audiences were to be treated to a pared-down performance that consisted of Elton and his piano. At an after-show party he chats with TV star David Soul. Notice the regrowth of Elton's hair following transplant treatment.

Live in LA

Opposite and above: Elton's return to Los Angeles saw him performing at the Universal Amphitheater, where he had last appeared in 1975. The tour was a success but much of the audience comprised loyal fans, rather than a new, younger base. Although Elton had released another new album, *Victim of Love*, his fans were more keen on listening to the old hits born out of his relationship with Bernie.

Ten years of success

Opposite: Back in sequins, Elton performs at MCA Records' party held at Hollywood's Palomino Club in honor of his ten years in the business. Elton was keen to restart his career as the new decade turned; in 1980 he released the album *21 at 33*, which referred to the fact that at only 33 years old he had already recorded 21 albums. He also staged another massive US tour, complete with Donald Duck and Minnie Mouse outfits and a huge free gig in New York's Central Park. Elton also left MCA to join the Geffen label.

Above: "Sharon" (left) and "Phyllis" (center) spotted out on the town in 1980. Elton and Rod Stewart's friendship had endured for over ten years, despite the occasional public squabble. They are seen here accompanied by Rod's wife, Alana Hamilton.

Working with Thom Bell

Opposite: Elton jumped at the chance to work with the Grammy award-winning producer Thom Bell, and their collaboration saw them record a number of tracks which were eventually released in album format as *The Complete Thom Bell Sessions*. Elton often credits Bell with having given him vital voice coaching, particularly for encouraging him to sing in a lower register.

Above: In the recording studio. Elton's first album with Geffen was *The Fox*, a slightly tentative album which saw Elton and Bernie writing together again but also featured material by Tom Robinson and Gary Osborne.

Back on tour

During late 1982 Elton takes to the stage for another big US tour. Most of the newer material came from the recently released album *Jump Up*, which included tracks such as the hit "Blue Eyes" and "Princess," the tune he reportedly wrote for his new friend, Princess Diana.

In costume

Above: Elton sports yet another specially designed hat—one of a series of oversized and overembellished NYPD caps. It seemed that Elton's love of absurd stage costumes was back.

Opposite: Elton appears in another flamboyant costume at Madison Square Garden in 1982. During the early eighties Elton gradually gathered his former bandmates around him, as well as beginning to work again with Bernie Taupin. The result was a return to Elton's successful earlier sound, and although he was no longer a teen idol, he was finally beginning to enjoy growing popularity.

Empty Garden

Above: Elton seen with Liza Minnelli before appearing on stage at New York's Madison Square Garden. It was Elton's first performance at the venue since the death of his friend John Lennon, and at the end of his tribute song, "Empty Garden," he was joined on stage by Lennon's widow, Yoko Ono, and her son—and Elton's godchild—Sean.

Opposite: The classic straw boater would become Elton's signature look for the next few years.

Still Standing

By 1984, Elton had proved that he was still standing. The 1983 album *Too Low for Zero* confirmed his comeback; it was a hit on both sides of the Atlantic, spending 54 weeks on the *Billboard* chart and reaching number 7 in the UK. And it included a couple of Elton's more memorable hits: "I'm Still Standing" and "I Guess That's Why They Call it the Blues." Yet despite success in his professional life, Elton was now at the height of his alcohol and cocaine addiction.

A surprise engagement

Opposite: Elton surprised his friends as well as his fans when he announced his engagement to Renate Blauel in February 1984. German-born Renate had been one of the sound engineers in Elton's entourage during the Australian tour.

Above: The pair were married just four days later, on St. Valentine's day, at St. Mark's Church, Sydney, Australia, with John Reid acting as best man. Despite all the speculation surrounding their marriage, Elton and Renate remained together until their divorce in 1988.

A career highlight

Opposite: Elton, in his role as chairman of Watford Football Club, and Renate pictured during the singing of the Cup Final hymn "Abide with Me," prior to the FA Cup Final between Everton and Watford at Wembley Stadium, May 19, 1984. Althought Everton won the match 2-0, Elton subsequently said that this day was one of the happiest of his life.

Above: Elton stands in the center of the Wembley pitch.

Looking relaxed

Above: Elton John congratulates George Michael on winning the Ivor Novello Songwriter of the Year Award at London's Grosvenor House Hotel, March 13, 1985.

Opposite: Elton stops for a chat with singer Natalie Cole at Greenwich film studios where Elton is shooting a video in May 1985.

Live Aid

Left: It's July 13, 1985 and the date of the Live Aid Concerts. Backstage at Wembly Stadium, Elton and George Michael chat to their royal friend, Princess Diana. Elton had performed one of the later sets, ringing out hits such as "Bennie and the Jets," "Rocket Man," and "I'm Still Standing."

Opposite: Elton and Bernie celebrate receiving their own Ivor Novello Award in April, 1986. The awards are presented to songwriters and lyricists and are chosen by the British Academy of Songwriters, Composers, and Authors.

When in Paris...

Above: Elton appears with Renate wearing another famed creation: the Eiffel Tower boater that was specially designed for his 1987 Paris concert. Despite having toned down his appearance Elton could still be relied upon to appear in outrageous and eye-catching outfits. Many, including this boater, would be auctioned off by Elton in 1988 in a bid both to raise money and to create space in his overcrowded homes in London and Windsor.

Opposite: June 1986 and a collection of famous faces gather for the Prince's Trust 10th Anniversary Rock concert at Wembley, London. The concert was held to celebrate the charitable organization created by Prince Charles, and Elton can be seen in the center row, behind Paul McCartney and an enthroned Tina Turner. Behind him stands a young Bryan Adams.

Tour de Force

Opposite and right: Elton's Australian Tour de Force tour at the end of 1986 harked back to the Glam rock days of the midseventies. Here Elton appears to blend Tina Turner with Amadeus Mozart. Behind the scenes Elton was beginning to suffer with the throat problems which would eventually lead to surgery—and the loss of those famous high notes.

Taking control

Opposite: Elton hits rock bottom in 1990. Gone are the outfits from his performance years during the seventies and eighties, gone is his extensive and lovingly cataloged record collection. Elton shed his past in an effort to take control; but it was to be his incredible charitable efforts that would enable him to make sense of his life again.

Right: Pictured at the launch of London's Planet Hollywood restaurant with owner Sylvester Stallone.

Two Rooms

Opposite: In 1991, Elton and Bernie celebrated their creative partnership by releasing the album, *Two Rooms*. The title refers to their unusual working style, which involved their writing separately—in two rooms. Despite achieving success with other lyricists, Elton has always cherished the relationship he has with Bernie.

Above: Elton perfoms with Tom Fogerty of Creedence Clearwater Revival at the 1988 Hall of Fame Awards. Despite appearances, Elton was in the grip of a deep depression, still affected by drugs and alcohol dependence. His marriage to Renate had finally ended and he had taken the decision to clear out all of his possessions, publicly declaring a need to create space, but privately wanting to rid himself of "Elton." The comeback album released later that year was appropriately entitled *Reg Strikes Back*.

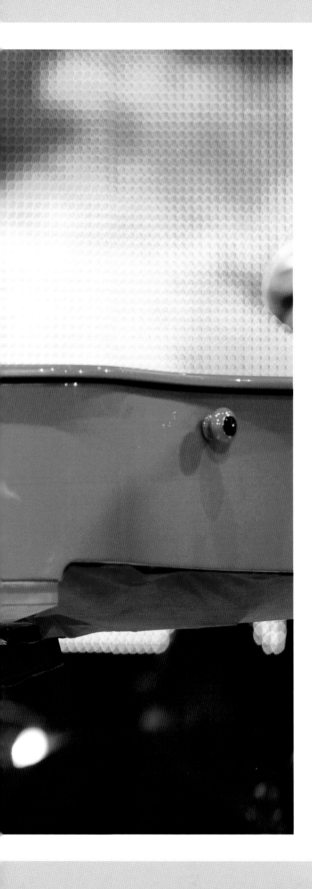

Chapter Four

To Be Continued

Don't Let the Sun Go Down on Me

Above: In early 1991 Elton had made a surprise guest appearance on stage with George Michael, and the two sang "Don't Let the Sun Go Down on Me," Elton's hit from 1974. The track was released as a single a few months later and by February 1992 it was Elton's first number 1 in the US for six years. The two then regularly appeared on stage together to perform the hit.

Opposite: Sharing a joke with the fashion designer Gianni Versace in May 1992. The Italian created a number of stunning performance outfits and stage sets for Elton, and the two became firm friends.

The Elton John Foundation

Above: Elton hosts a post-Oscars party in 1993, pictured here with winners Steven Speilberg and Tom Hanks. The party was a fundraiser for Elton's AIDS charity organization the Elton John Foundation. Deeply affected by the plight of a number of friends, including the young Ryan White, and by a personal need to apply himself to something beyond his music, Elton made the most of his celebrity connections and threw himself into fundraising.

Opposite: Onstage during the 1992 US tour. With a top ten album in the *Billboard* 200, high energy stage performances that harked back to earlier shows, and the hand of Versace in every design, the tour was a complete success.

Welcome to the Hall of Fame

Right: Elton and Bernie celebrate Elton's entry into the Rock and Roll Hall of Fame in 1994. Inductees only qualify for entry into the Hall of Fame when they have passed the milestone of 25 years since the release of their first record—a feat which the Captain and the Cowboy achieved in 1994. Although the honor was being bestowed upon Elton, he insisted that Bernie join him on stage, famously declaring that there would be no Elton John without Bernie Taupin. Bernie had already been inducted into the Songwriters Hall of Fame in 1992.

Opposite: April 1993: Elton appears at a concert to benefit the Gay Men's Health Crisis at the Nederlander Theater in New York. He is seen here with Smokey Robinson and Aretha Franklin. The concert, *Aretha Franklin: Duets*, was taped and broadcast on US television. Elton had come a long way from that first admission of his sexuality in *Rolling Stone* in 1976; his lifestyle was not only openly acknowledged and legitimate, but could also be used to benefit those in need. In October 1993 he would meet his life partner David Furnish.

Academy Award winners

Above: And the winner is ... Elton John and Tim Rice proudly show off their own Acadamy Awards in 1995. Their song, "Can You Feel the Love Tonight," was the Oscar winner. His collaboration with Rice on Disney's *The Lion King* was the greatest success Elton was to know with another lyricist. The musical was one of the highest grossing animated movies and spawned a number of hit songs, including "Circle of Life." Elton went on to win a Grammy for "Can You Feel the Love Tonight" and the soundrack album would eventually sell upwards of 15 million copies worldwide.

Opposite: Africa inspires Elton's zebra-print stage outfit in 1996.

Master performers

Master performers. Elton performed in Modena, Italy, at Luciano Pavarotti's charity concert Pavarotti and Friends. The opera maestro hosted the annual event in order to raise money for various UN causes and in 1996 Elton and Pavarotti's duet of "Live Like Horses" closed the show in spectacular style.

Times of sadness and joy

Opposite: Elton's 50th birthday celebrations, held at London's Hammersmith Palais, were typically lavish, with Elton dressed as Louis XIV of France and partner David Furnish as his consort. Elton's wig was reportedly so large and heavy that it forced the host to arrive at the party in a furniture truck!

Above: 1997 was to be a year of shocking loss for Elton. In July his great friend Gianni Versace was gunned down in Miami Beach. At the designer's funeral in Milan, Elton was comforted by Princess Diana; the two friends had allegedly disagreed of late and their shared grief brought them back together. On Elton's left is his other "rock," his partner David Furnish.

Candle in the Wind

Opposite: Just weeks later Elton attends another high profile funeral, that of Princess Diana. Following her sudden death, Bernie rewrote the lyrics to "Candle in the Wind"; at the request of the Royal Family, the song was performed in Westminster Abbey before a worldwide audience of some one billion people. On its release it became the UK's fastest selling single and debuted at number 1 in the US, selling 3.5 million copies in the first week of its release alone. It went on to become the highest selling single worldwide of all time.

Above: Elton almost missed Diana's funeral, so deep was his depression at losing two friends in such quick succession. The support of others was key to his attendance and his performance that day; l–r, George Michael, Elton, and David Furnish.

An all-star lineup

Opposite: Elton enjoys an evening with rap star Sean Combs (P. Diddy) and Donatella Versace, sister of Gianni. In 1997, Elton became the subject of a documentary directed by his partner, David Furnish. Titled *Tantrums and Tiaras*, the film was a warts-and-all exposure of the "real" Elton, showing both his sensitive and his more temperamental sides.

Above: The all-star lineup for the 1997 Rainforest Foundation concert at New York's Carnegie Hall, l–r: Zucchero, Bobby McFerrin, Jimmy Nail, James Taylor, Trudie Styler, Elton, Lyle Lovett, Bonnie Raitt, Stevie Wonder, Shawn Colvin, and Sting.

Good times and bad times

Opposite: February, 1998: Elton receives his knighthood with his family beside him: mum Sheila, stepfather Fred, and life partner David.

Above: At a Whitehouse state dinner in honor of visiting Prime Minister Tony Blair, guest performers Elton and Stevie Wonder are thanked by President Bill Clinton. Behind the scenes Elton was dealing with a breakdown in relations with his former manager and partner John Reid. The two were now facing each other in court over financial irregularities and the ensuing media frenzy exposed some of Elton's more extravagant spending habits.

Swingtime!

Above: Swingtime! Elton duets with Tony Bennett at the 1999 Rainforest Foundation Concert.

Opposite: Having already successfully moved from screen to the Broadway stage, the theater version of *The Lion King* premiered in London in October 1999. Elton, pictured here at the premiere with former Spice Girl Geri Haliwell, had recently been fitted with a pacemaker to correct an irregular heartbeat.

A special Grammy

Opposite: A special award at the Grammys for Elton in February 2000. He was presented with the Person of the Year trophy, in part for his contribution to the music industry, but also as recognition of his charitable works. With him is his regular performing partner, Billy Joel.

Above: In October 2000 Elton staged a series of "one night only" gigs at Madison Square Garden to showcase his and Bernie's back catalogue of hits. Joined on stage by a number of his star friends, here he is seen with Anastasia, with whom he sang "Saturday Night's Alright For Fighting."

Old friends

Elton is joined by old friend Kiki Dee. The two not only had "Don't Go Breaking My Heart" to perform but also their single "True Love," from 1992. Tapes of the concerts were pressed into a live album and DVD package.

Illustrious company

Opposite: Pictured with Brazilian football legend Pelé in November 2000. Meanwhile Elton was celebrating the success of yet another Broadway hit, *Aida*, another collaboration with the newly knighted Tim Rice.

Above: Elton and David attend a dinner at St. James's Palace held to celebrate 25 years of the Prince's Trust, the foundation created by Prince Charles to support disadvantaged young people in the UK.

Honored by the Academy of Music

Above: At an all-star tribute to Brian Wilson, Elton performs with Billy Joel and Paul Simon. The event came just weeks after Elton's surprise performance with the controversial rapper Eminem at the Grammys. Appearing with Billy Joel was far more usual; the two spent much of 2001 touring together with "Face 2 Face."

Opposite: Elton, pictured here with his mother and stepfather, is honored with a First Honorary Doctorate of Music from the prestigious Royal Academy of Music. Although Elton had attended the academy when still a precocious young talent, he had left before completing his degree. His classical training had certainly influenced much of the music he composed with both Bernie and Tim Rice, which often lent itself to more complex and orchestral arrangements.

Fundraiser

At a fundraising concert for AIDS charities, Elton croons in the company of Jon Bon Jovi. By late 2001 Elton had released *Songs from the West Coast*, which performed well in the UK charts, peaking at number 2. He had also performed at the Madison Square Garden post-9/11 benefit, the Concert for New York. Appearing alongside such names as Janet Jackson, The Who, Mick Jagger and Keith Richards, and Paul McCartney, Elton sang "I Want Love" and "Mona Lisas and Mad Hatters" before duetting with Billy Joel on "Your Song."

The White Tie and Tiara Ball

Above: First held in 1999, Elton's now famous celebrity-rich White Tie and Tiara Ball is an annual event held at his mansion, Woodside. Here at the 1991 party Elton shows off the diamond studded Chopard watch which, when auctioned by Kevin Spacey later in the evening, prompted a good natured bidding war with actress Kate Winslet.

Opposite: Regular guests at Woodside, David and Victoria Beckham enjoy an evening of fine dining, top class entertainment, and eventually breakfast at the White Tie and Tiara Ball. The dress code at the event is always the same no matter what the theme: white tie and tails for men, ballgown and tiara for the ladies. Since its inception, the ball has raised over £40 million for the Elton John AIDS Foundation.

Working hard

Opposite: Sir Elton poses with Dame Judi Dench at his fifth White Tie and Tiara event. Notice David Furnish's distinctly dapper tuxedo; the ball had a 1930s theme in 2003, inspired by the movie *Gosford Park*. During the evening auction Elton sold an autographed piano and at one point during the proceedings £1,000,000 was raised in just 20 minutes.

Above: As part of a series of TV interviews in the US, Elton appears on *The Tonight Show* to chat to Jay Leno. He also found himself on *The Ellen Degeneres Show* and *The Sharon Osbourne Show*, all during October. 2003 had been a hectic year for Elton, with almost nonstop touring, benefit gigs, and TV appearances. He also achieved another chart hit with the remix of "Are You Ready for Love." First recorded during the Thom Bell sessions of 1977, it reached the top spot in the UK, providing Elton with a number 1 in each of the four decades of his career.

A staggering sum

Elton and Rod Stewart perform during Andre Agassi's Grand
Slam for Children benefit concert at the MGM Grand Garden Arena
in Las Vegas in September 2002. The event raised a staggering
$5.6 million for the tennis player's charity foundation.

That's entertainment!

James Taylor, Rebekah Del Rio, Sting, and Elton go all out to entertain the crowd at the 12th Annual Rainforest Foundation concert in New York, 2002. Sting had founded the charity in 1989 in order to raise money and awareness for the indigenous tribes of the Amazon.

Billy Elliot

Opposite: 2005 saw the opening of Elton's next venture into musical theater, Billy Elliot: The Musical, for which he wrote the music to accompany Lee Hall's lyrics. He is pictured here with the show's director, Stephen Daldry, at the press launch, held at the Royal Academy of Music. Despite costing over £5 million to stage, the show was an instant critical and commercial success and went on to win four prestigious Laurence Olivier awards.

Above: Elton poses with the three actors who shared the title role in Billy Elliot, l–r: Liam Mower, George McGuire, and James Lomas.

Raising awareness

Above: Elton and David pose with the photographer Mario Testino (center) at the launch of a book aimed at raising awareness for women living with HIV/AIDS, *Women to Women: Positively Speaking*. The photographs found within its pages are by Testino. David Furnish's interest in the visual arts led to his taking a lead role in Rocket Pictures, the production company that he and Elton had set up in 1996.

Opposite: Elton in Las Vegas, 2002.

Kennedy Center Honor

Opposite: In December 2004 Elton was awarded a prestigious Kennedy Center honor. Alongside him are the other recipients of the award, l–r (back): Warren Beatty, Ossie Davis, John Williams; (front): Elton, Ruby Dee, Joan Sutherland. Awarded to exponents of the performing arts, the honors have the gravitas of a British knighthood; following the ceremony at the US Department of State, Elton and his fellow honorees were treated to a reception at the White House.

Above: Elton's live performances continued unabated during 2004. Here he is pictured during one of four shows at London's Hammersmith Apollo.

Raising funds through sport

Above: Friends for many years, Billie Jean King and Elton act as coaches for the two teams participating in the Advanta WTT Smash Hits celebrity tennis match to benefit the Elton John AIDS Foundation at the Bren Center at UC Irvine on September 14, 2006.

Opposite Elton high-fives teammate Serena Williams during the 2009 competition, which took place at Baton Rouge.

Tsunami single

Opposite: The calamitous tsunami that hit Asia on Boxing Day 2004 prompted the pop fraternity to release another benefit single. "Tears in Heaven," penned by Eric Clapton, was recorded in January of 2005 in London; Elton is seen here with rock guitarist and fellow contributor Slash.

Above: Arriving at another charity function with David Furnish and Diana Krall; this time it's for the Elton John AIDS Foundation, and the event is the launch of a book featuring photographs of famous women wearing nothing but Jimmy Choo shoes and a single piece of Cartier jewelry.

BOB GELDOF

HARVEY GOLDSMITH

Live 8

Above: The Live 8 concerts took place in July 2005, 20 years after the original Live Aid spectacular and designed to coincide not only with the anniversary but also with the G8 summit, which was to be held in Scotland just days later. The assembled team of organizers resembled those who had engineered the earlier event. Sir Bob Geldof (far right) and Midge Ure (center left), both of whom had organized Live Aid, are joined by Elton and the former French culture minister Jack Lang (center right) to announce the details.

Opposite: At the free concert, staged in London's Hyde Park, Elton performed "The Bitch is Back" and "Saturday Night's Alright for Fighting," then went on to duet with UK pop singer Pete Doherty on T-Rex's "Children of the Revolution."

Making a commitment

Above: The personal highlight of Elton's year was almost certainly his civil partnership "marriage" to David Furnish. Passed as an Act of Parliament in the UK in 2004, civil partnership gave same sex couples the same rights and responsibilities as those embarking on civil marriage. Elton and David led the way when they were married in their hometown of Old Windsor on the very first day that such partnerships could be celebrated. The ceremony itself was small and private, attended only by close family and friends; it was the lavish party later on that saw a huge gathering of celebrity guests at Woodside, bringing Windsor to a halt.

Opposite: Overlooked by fellow singer Celine Dion, a newly married Elton sits at his famous red piano, during his residency at the Colosseum at Caesars Palace, Las Vegas. The Red Piano tour first began in 2004 and was a huge success; in 2006 it ran from January to April.

Remembering Diana

Opposite: Another anniversary, this time the 10th anniversary of the death of Diana, Princess of Wales. Elton and David arrive at the service of thanksgiving alongside Camilla al Fayed, the sister of Diana's partner, Dodi.

Above: Elton arrives on stage at the memorial concert to be greeted by Diana's sons, Princes William and Harry. As hosts and organizers of the event, they had requested that Elton play. The only notable absence was any performance of "Candle in the Wind 1997"; Elton had once said he would only ever repeat his performance from Westminster Abbey should the princes ask him to.

60 years young

Opposite: Still standing after all this time. Seen here on stage in Riga, Elton shows that he still has what
it takes. In March of 2007 Elton celebrated his 60th birthday with a huge concert at Madison Square
Garden. The performance and the after party became the subject of a TV documentary and a DVD release.

Above: Elton and long-standing band member Davey Johnstone on stage in Austin, Texas.

Broadway success

Above: The success of *Billy Elliot* in London inevitably led to its opening on Broadway. On November 13, 2008, the award winning team were there to celebrate the first night. L–r: Stephen Daldry, Elton, Lee Hall, and David Furnish.

Opposite: At the curtain call of the opening night, Elton appeared on stage dressed in a tutu to take a bow. He is accompanied by that night's lead actor, Kiril Kulish, plus cast members. The show was a triumph and went on to scoop an impressive 15 Tony award nominations.

Still rocking

In April 2009 Elton's Red Piano Tour came to a close in Las Vegas. Elton played 241 concerts in the 4,300-seat showroom, with a setlist composed of almost all of his most beloved hits. Its success, in both Nevada and then Europe provided proof of Elton's enduring popularity on both sides of the Atlantic, no mean feat for a musician whose career began four decades earlier. Although the 2009 European tour was interrupted due to Elton's having fallen ill, he showed every intention of returning to the stage in 2010, releasing concert dates that promised his fans the return of the Rocket Man.

Chronology

1947

March 25: Reginald Kenneth Dwight is born in the London suburb of Pinner.

1958

Wins a scholarship to the Royal Acadamy of Music, aged 11. Reg left the Academy five years later.

1964

Forms the band Bluesology and begins to play in pubs and clubs across England.

1967

June: Having responded to an ad looking for new talent in Britain's *New Musical Express* Elton meets and teams up with Bernie Taupin.

Reg Dwight becomes Elton Hercules John—not officially changing his name until later.

1968

Elton and Bernie become staff songwriters for Dick James Music.

1969

June: *Empty Sky*, Elton's first album, is released in England, under the Dick James Label, DJM. The album wasn't released in the US until 1975, when it reached number 8 in the *Billboard* chart.

1970

August 25: Elton's performing debut is in America at Los Angeles' Troubadour nightclub.

Released on both sides of the Atlantic sinultaneously, *Elton John* peaked at number 4 in the States and number 5 in the UK.

1971

January: "Your Song" reaches number 8 in UK singles chart.

Again on the DJM label, *Tumbleweed Connection* performs well, peaking in the UK at number 2.

It is followed by two further albums that year, *11-17-70* and *Madman Across the Water*. Both are well received, but neither album reaches the top spot.

1972

July: the single "Rocket Man" reaches number 6.

Honky Chateau on the Uni / DJM label becomes Elton's first US number 1 album.

Elton founds his own recording label, Rocket Records, and goes on to sign a number of young, aspiring acts.

1973

January: *Don't Shoot Me, I'm Only the Piano Player* becomes Elton's second straight number one in the US and yields two classic singles: "Crocodile Rock" which is Elton's first number 1 single and "Daniel."

October: The double album *Goodbye Yellow Brick Road* is released by MCA (US) and DJM (UK). Reaching number 1 in both the US and the UK, it spent over 100 weeks on the *Billboard* Pop charts and sold over 30 million copies. It remains Elton's best selling studio album.

1974

The chart topping *Caribou* was released in June by MCA/DJM, spending 54 weeks in the US charts, but only 18 weeks in the UK.

The single "Don't Let the Sun Go Down on Me" features Beach Boys Carl Wilson and Bruce Johnston on backing vocals.

November: Elton is joined onstage by John Lennon for a performance of "Whatever Gets You Through the Night" at Madison Square Garden. It turns out to be Lennon's last live performance.

1975

The first of Elton's compilation albums, *Elton John: Greatest Hits,* also reached number 1 and became Elton's best selling album to date, selling over 32 million copies worldwide.

Released in May by MCA/DJM, *Captain Fantastic and the Brown Dirt Cowboy* became the first album to ever debut at number 1 on the US pop charts.

Rock of the Westies was released in October, and it too debuted at number 1 in the US. It fared less well in the UK, reaching only number 5.

Elton appears in the film *Tommy* and performs a hit cover version of "Pinball Wizard."

1976

August: Elton's duet with Kiki Dee, "Don't Go Breaking My Heart" tops the charts for the first of four weeks. It is his last one in the US for 21 years.

The live album *Here and There* consisting of recorded performances from London's Royal Festival Hall ('Here') and New York's Madison Square Garden ('There') peaked at number 4 in the US and number 7 in the UK.

Blue Moves released by MCA (US) and Rocket Records (UK) was

Elton's second double album. It peaked at number 3 on both sides of the Atlantic.

Elton declares in an interview with *Rolling Stone* magazine that he is bisexual.

1977

November: An exhausted Elton announces at a London concert that he is retiring from live performances, which he does—for 15 months.

The second of his compilation albums, *Elton John: Greatest Hits Vol. 2,* fails to fare as well as its predecessor. It peaks at only number 21 in the US and number 6 at home.

1978

A Single Man is Elton's first album to be released without any creative input from either Bernie Taupin or Elton's regular producer, Gus Dudgeon. It reached number 15 on the *Billboard* chart and number 8 in the UK.

1979

The Thom Bell Sessions was released by MCA in the US, two years after it had been recorded. Originally consisting of only three tracks, on its re-release in 1989 three further tracks were added. Elton John resumes touring after a 15-month hiatus.

Elton becomes the first Western pop star to tour the Soviet Union.

Victim of Love released in October by MCA/ Rocket Records.

1980

May: Elton John releases *21 at 33*, which reunites him with Bernie Taupin. The title refers to the fact that it is the 33-year-old Elton's 21st album.

1981

The Fox on the Geffen label in the US and Rocket Records in the US. It reaches number 21 in the *Billboard* charts. In the UK it peaks at number 12.

1982

In April, *Jump Up!* reaches 17 and 13 in the US and UK charts respectively.

1983

June: *Too Low for Zero* sees Bernie Taupin writing the lyrics to all of Elton's tracks again. The album performs better in the UK, where it peaks at number 7. It reaches number 25 on the *Billboard* charts.

1984

Breaking Hearts again sees greater success on home soil, achieving a chart position of number 2 in the UK and number 20 in the US.

February: Elton marries his sound engineer, Renate Blauel, in a surprise ceremony in Australia. The marriage lasts until 1988.

1985

Produced by returning Gus Dudgeon and released on the Geffen and Rocket labels, *Ice on Fire* reaches number 3 in the UK, and 48 in the US.

July: Elton performs onstage at London's Wembley Stadium for Live Aid.

1986

November: *Leather Jackets* is released on the Geffen/Rocket Records label.

Elton begins to suffer with throat problems and temporarily loses his voice. Surgery to his vocal chords results in the loss of his famous falsetto.

1987

Elton's return to the MCA label in the US, sees former record label, Geffen release the compilation album *Elton John: Greatest Hits Vol. 3*.

August: Elton switches on the channel to launch MTV Europe.

1988

Reg Strikes Back on the MCA/Rocket Records labels peaks at number 16 in the US and number 18 in the UK. It fares even better in Europe, where Italian fans place the album at number 3 in their charts.

November: Elton concludes a sold-out five-night stand at Madison Square Garden. Being his 26th sold-out concert at the venue, it breaks the house record set by the Grateful Dead.

1989

Sleeping With the Past is released and dedicated to Bernie. Despite not being a critical success it does spawn Elton's first solo UK number 1 single, "Sacrifice."

1990

To Be Continued released by MCA and Rocket Records is a box-set compilation of Elton's music from his days in Bluesology to the present. Running at over 5 hours in length it contained over 70 of Elton's best tracks.

The Very Best of Elton John is another compilation album, this time focusing on Elton greatest hits. Released in the UK on the Polygram label it spent two weeks at number one then a further 143 weeks within the top 200.

His long-standing addiction to drugs and alcohol is addressed when Elton finally checks in to a rehab clinic in Chicago.

1991

The compilation album *Two Rooms* is released with an accompanying documentary, all of which focuses on Elton and Bernie's unique working relationship.

1992

The One becomes the first album to receive official multi-platinum certification from the Recording Industry Association of America and is Elton's best selling album in the States since 1975.

Rare Masters, a compilation of B-sides and outtakes, is released by Polydor.

Elton and Bernie are inducted into the Songwriters' Hall of Fame.

Elton performs a duet with Axl Rose of "Bohemian Rhapsody" at the Freddy Mercury memorial concert in London.

December: The Elton John AIDS Foundation is established.

1993

Duets is a compilation of Elton tracks performed by himself and a chosen artist. Released by MCA and Rocket, it reached number 5 in the UK and number 25 in the US.

April: The charting on *Billboard*'s Top Forty of "Simple Life" breaks the record set by Elvis for 24 consecutive years of Top Forty hits.

Elton meets Canadian advertising executive David Furnish, who becomes his long-term partner.

1994

January: Elton is inducted into the Rock and Roll Hall of Fame.

The Lion King is released on the Disney record label. Elton composes the music, alongside lyricist Tim Rice, for Disney's smash hit animation. The single "Can You Feel the Love Tonight" peaks in the US Top Forty at number 4, extending Elton's record-breaking streak of consecutive years of Top Forty hits to 25.

1995

Made in England is released in the UK by Rocket and in the US on the Island label. It achieves a number 3 position in the UK album charts, again bettering in performance in the US; however the single "Believe" broke into the US top twenty.

March: Elton receives a Grammy Award for "Can You Feel the Love Tonight." Three weeks later the same song recieves an Oscar for Best Song from a Motion Picture.

1996

Love Songs also performs well on home territory reaching number 4.

1997

The Big Picture released by Rocket and A&M Records in September was dedicated to the recently deceased Gianni Versace. It fared reasonably well on both sides of the Atlantic reaching number 9 Stateside and number 3 at home.

September: Elton plays a tribute performance of 'Candle in the Wind' at the Westminster Abbey funeral of Princess Diana.

October: 'Candle in the Wind 1997' becomes the biggest-selling single worldwide in chart history.

1998

Elton receives a knighthood at Buckingham Palace. From now on he is known as Sir Elton John.

Teams up with Tim Rice to write the songbook for *Aida* for which the two would later win a Tony Award.

1999

Elton John and Tim Rice's Aida is the album of the music from the show. Elton performs the music alongside a number of other performers; it is not a recording of the original cast.

The Muse, a soundtrack album, is released by Polydor.

2000

Elton's working relationship with Disney continues with the soundtrack album, *The Road to Eldorado* which is released in March.

One Night Only, a compilation of greatest hits, but this time recorded live from his performance at Madison Square Garden, is released.

2001

October: *Songs from the West Coast* is released on the Universal (US) and Rocket labels and reaches numbers 15 in the US and 2 in the UK.

2002

The comprehensive *Greatest Hits 1970-2002* was released by Universal, who now owned the rights to the Elton John catalogue. It debuted at number 12 in the US and eventually reached number 3 in the UK.

Elton receives his honorary doctorate from the Royal Academy of Music.

2004

Peachtree Road, Elton's 28th Studio album was released in November by Universal and Rocket Records.

Elton and the band begin their 'Red Piano' residency at the Caesars Palace Colosseum in Las Vegas.

2005

Elton and Bernie collaborate on the music for the Broadway production of *Lestat*.

December: Elton and David Furnish marry in a Civil Partnership ceremony in London.

Billy Elliot the Musical opens in London. The music is provided by Elton. The production goes on to win four Laurence Olivier Awards.

2006

The Captain and the Kid released by Interscope Records (US) and Mercury, reached number 6 in the UK and number 18 in the US.

Elton is named a 'Disney Legend'.

2007

Released on the Mercury label, *Rocket Man: Number Ones* is released in March to celebrate Elton's 60th birthday.

March: Elton celebrates his 60th birthday with a record-breaking 60th appearance at New York's Madison Square Garden.

Elton's entire back catalogue of almost 500 tracks becomes available to legally download.

2008

Billy Elliot the Musical opens on Broadway.

2009

Billy Elliot the Musical wins 10 Tony Awards.